AMAZING HISTORY

LOST CITIES

NEIL MORRIS

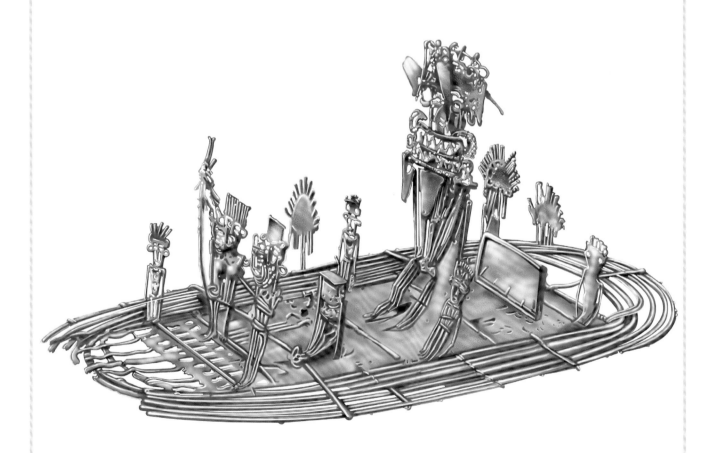

W
FRANKLIN WATTS

 An Appleseed Editions book

First published in 2007 by Franklin Watts

Franklin Watts
338 Euston Road, London NW1 3BH

Franklin Watts Australia
Level 17/207 Kent St, Sydney, NSW 2000

© 2007 Appleseed Editions

Appleseed Editions Ltd
Well House, Friars Hill, Guestling, East Sussex TN35 4ET

Created by Q2A Media
Series Editor: Jean Coppendale
Designers: Diksha Khatri, Ashita Murgai
Picture Researchers: Lalit Dalal, Jyoti Sachdev
Illustrators: Hemant Arya, Subhash Vohra, Rajesh Das, Kumari Rupa Singh

ISBN   978 0 7496 7538 7

Dewey classification: 001.94

All words in **bold** can be found in the glossary on page 30.

Website information is correct at time of going to press. However, the publishers cannot
accept liability for any information or links found on third-party websites.

A CIP catalogue for this book is available from the British Library.

Picture Credits:
t=top b=bottom c=centre l=left r=right m=middle
Cover images:
Back cover:
Peter Arnold Images Inc/ Photolibrary: 4b, Index Stock Imagery/ Photolibrary: 5t, Bettmann/ Corbis: 5b, 13, The Bridgeman Art
Library/ Photolibrary: 6b, 7t, 12b, 14b, 22b, Super Stock: 7b, J.M. Kenoyer, Courtesy Dept. of Archaeology and Museums,
Govt. of Pakistan: 8b, Arcturus Publishing Limited: 9t, 9b, Koster/ Shutterstock: 10b, John Hua/ Shutterstock: 15t, Dhuss/
Istockphoto: 15b, John Lee/ Istockphoto: 16b, Lim Beng Lay/ Shutterstock: 17b, Jackhynes: 18b, Gordon Galbraith/
Shutterstock: 19t, Michael Puerzer/ Istockphoto: 19b, Robin Smith/ Photolibrary: 20b, David Reed/ Corbis: 21t, Q2A Media:
21b, 23t, Bill Bachmann Photography/ Photolibrar: 24b, Illustrations by Robert Frederick Ltd: 25bl, Toon Possemiers/
Istockphoto: 25br, Garry Peck/ Shutterstock: 26b, Robert Harding Picture Library Ltd/ Photolibrary: 28b, gray goodfleisch/
Istockphoto: 29t, National Aeronautics and Space Administration (NASA): 29b.

Printed in China

Franklin Watts is a division of Hachette Children's Books

Contents

What is a lost city?

Imagine you are hacking through a dense rainforest or trekking across a vast desert. Suddenly you come across some old ruins. Could this be a lost city? Lost cities are what is left of large, ancient **settlements** and are found all over the world.

Digging up the past

How were cities 'lost'? Why did the people who lived there leave? War, famine, earthquake or flood may have driven them away. **Archaeologists** searching for remains from the past, look for parts of buildings, graves or tools. This evidence contains vital clues about how people lived long ago and helps to solve the mystery of why a city was abandoned and left to fall into ruins.

When they make a find, archaeologists dig up the ancient remains, examine them and try to fit them together.

The name Babylon came from a word meaning 'gateway of the gods'. This blue gate at Babylon was dedicated to Ishtar, goddess of love and war.

HOTSPOTS

As well as its ceremonial gate, Babylon is famous for its Hanging Gardens. These were listed as one of the Seven Wonders of the Ancient World, but their remains have never been found.

The Hanging Gardens overlooked the River Euphrates, which was used to water them.

Wonder of the world

Babylon was once one of the most important cities in Mesopotamia. Its remains lie in what is present-day Iraq. Babylon was built about 4,000 years ago and fell to ruin about 2,000 years later. The city was rediscovered less than 200 years ago by scholars searching for the Tower of Babel mentioned in the Bible.

Ur – the forgotten city

Ur, one of the world's oldest cities, was built over 5,000 years ago in present-day Iraq. It was once really powerful, but for thousands of years it remained lost and forgotten.

The ziggurat

In 1854, archaeologists discovered the remains of a building called a **ziggurat** and realized they had found the site of the city of Ur. The ziggurat was built in about 2100 BC, during the reign of King Ur-Nammu. The mud-brick structure was a type of stepped pyramid with a temple to the Moon-god Nanna at the top. The ziggurat was designed to represent a mountain reaching up to the gods.

Stairway to the gods
A golden statue of the god Nanna was carried up the stairs to the temple once a year

Platforms
The tower was made of three platforms, one on top of the other

This modern reconstruction shows what the ziggurat looked like. The building was at the centre of the city, with palaces and cemeteries around it.

Buried alive

In the 1920s, British archaeologist Leonard Woolley **excavated** Ur. He worked for five years and found nothing. Then suddenly he made some amazing discoveries. In the underground burial chambers of the royal graveyard, he found the remains of processions of animals pulling wheeled vehicles, as well as the skeletons of men and women. Their decorated headdresses and the remains of their clothes showed that the people were royal servants, soldiers and musicians.

Strings

Originally these may have been made of fibre, **gut** or wire

This lyre (a type of harp) has been rebuilt from remains found at the site.

HOTSPOTS

In one tomb lay the bodies of 68 women wearing gold jewellery and six men guarding the door. There were no signs of violence. They must have gone into the tomb, happy to be chosen to die with their king.

Procession

People, animals and chariots make their way to the city

This mosaic panel was found in the royal cemetery. It is made of pink stone, shell and a decorative blue stone called lapis lazuli.

Mohenjo-Daro

Near the banks of the River Indus stand the ruins of Mohenjo-Daro, also known as the Mound of the Dead, a city built more than 4,000 years ago.

Planned city streets

Mohenjo-Daro, in present-day Pakistan, was divided into two parts – a fortified **citadel** set on a mound with important public buildings, and a lower area of houses. The streets were laid out in a **grid** pattern and had covered drains for sewage. Mud-brick houses had rooms on two storeys around a courtyard. They also had a bathroom and a toilet.

Pakistan

Mohenjo-Daro India

This bearded figure is carved from a soft rock called steatite, or soapstone. It is one of many objects archaeologists found on the site of Mohenjo-Daro.

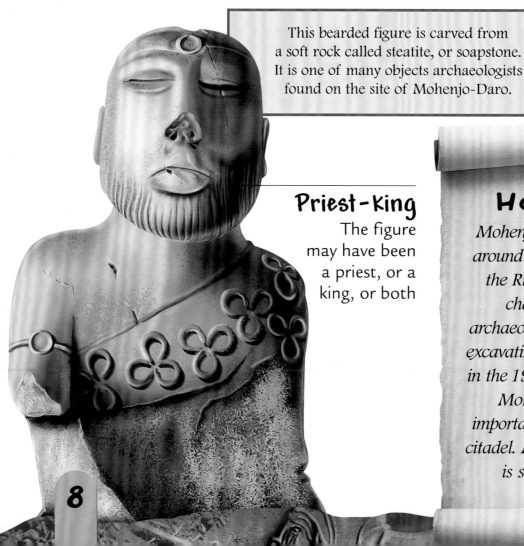

Priest-King
The figure may have been a priest, or a king, or both

HOTSPOTS

Mohenjo-Daro was abandoned around 1700 BC, probably when the River Indus unexpectedly changed course. Indian archaeologist R.D. Banerji started excavating the city in 1921. Later, in the 1950s, British archaeologist Mortimer Wheeler found important public buildings in the citadel. Many people believe there is still more to be found.

Bathtime

The Great Bath in the citadel looks like an open-air swimming pool. But experts think it was not used for fun, but for **ritual** bathing before worshipping the **Indus gods**. The bath measured 12 x 7 metres and was made of baked brick, sealed with **bitumen** to make it waterproof. It was filled to a depth of 2.5 metres with water from a well next door. About 5,000 people may have lived in the citadel.

Carved tablets like this were used by traders in Mahenjo-Daro to seal, or mark, goods. This seal shows a bull and has writing on it that no one has been able to decipher. Thousands of seals were found among the ruins of the city.

Steps
Lead down to the water

Brick walls
Line the bath, which was filled with water and could be drained

The Great Bath was at the centre of the citadel.

Knossos

Ancient Greek legends tell of King Minos who kept a Minotaur – a monster with the body of a man and the head of a bull – in an underground **labyrinth**, or maze, on the Greek island of Crete.

The palace of King Minos

In 1900, British archaeologist Arthur Evans went to Crete where he discovered the wonders of the city of Knossos. He found a palace with a maze of corridors. The ruins reminded him of the myth of King Minos and the Minotaur, so Evans named the people who lived there **Minoans**, after the King.

Italy
Greece
Crete •**Knossos**

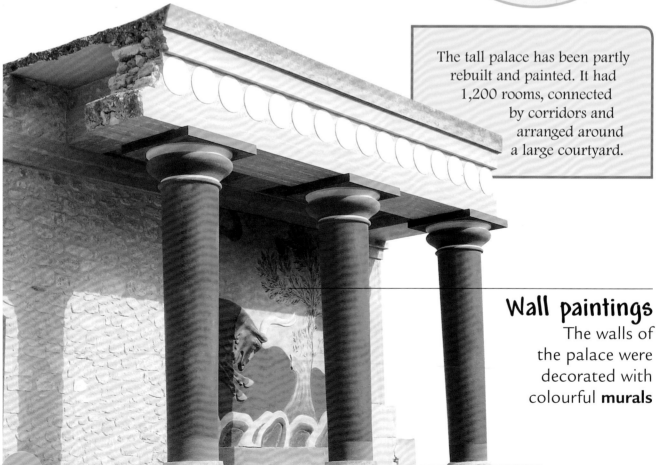

The tall palace has been partly rebuilt and painted. It had 1,200 rooms, connected by corridors and arranged around a large courtyard.

Wall paintings
The walls of the palace were decorated with colourful **murals**

Leaping the bull

The Minoans honoured and worshipped bulls. We know from wall-paintings that they also enjoyed the dangerous ritual, or sport, of bull-leaping. Bulls and bull-leapers were also found on Minoan seals, ornaments, vases and cups. Historians believe that the palace courtyard was used as a training ground for these amazing gymnastics.

HOTSPOTS

Knossos was toppled in about 1470 BC when a volcano erupted on the nearby island of Thira. A hundred years later the palace burned out completely and the city was taken over by warriors from the Greek mainland.

Long horns

Cretan bulls were known for their long, dangerous horns

A wall painting from the palace at Knossos. The red leaping figure is a young man, and the attendants are female. These acrobatics may have been part of an athletic competition.

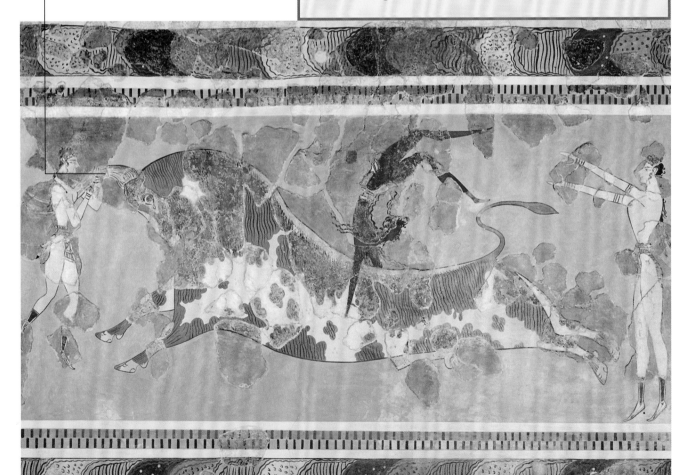

Troy

The walled city of ancient Troy stood on a hilltop protected by a strong, brick wall. The ancient Greek poet, Homer, told of a war that took place more than 3,000 years ago between the Trojans (people of Troy) and the Greeks.

In search of a dream

Heinrich Schliemann (1822–90), a German archaeologist, was determined to find the lost city of Troy. In 1870, he began digging with 100 Turkish workmen at Hissarlik, on the west coast of Turkey. They found not one but nine buried cities, each built on top of the one below. Schliemann dug through the ruins of each city and, near the bottom, discovered thick walls, well-built houses, and gold and silver jewellery.

The mask of Agamemnon. Schliemann thought he had discovered the body of the legendary Greek leader and named the mask after him. Research has shown it comes from an earlier time.

HOTSPOTS

Schliemann said that he decided to search for Troy when he first read the Iliad, *a story by Homer, when he was eight years old. He made a huge fortune dealing in gold in California, and then devoted the rest of his life and money to finding the city.*

The wooden horse

According to Homer, the Trojan War began when Paris, the son of King Priam of Troy, stole Helen, the beautiful wife of a Greek king and took her back to his city. The Greeks swore revenge and **besieged** Troy for ten years. In the end they tricked the Trojans into accepting a gift of a large wooden horse. Greek soldiers were hidden inside the horse, and when the Trojans were asleep the soldiers crept out, opened the city gates and let in the Greek army. Troy was destroyed and disappeared without trace until the 19th century.

Many historians, artists and film-makers have imagined the size and look of the wooden horse. About 30 soldiers are thought to have been in the horse.

Pompeii

Pompeii is one of the most famous archaeological sites in the world. For hundreds of years it lay buried under deep layers of volcanic ash.

Run for your lives!

The morning of 24 August, AD 79, was like any other summer's day. But suddenly there was an explosion and the ground began to shake. Smoke rose from nearby Mount Vesuvius, cloaking everything in darkness, and the people of Pompeii ran for their lives. About 2,000 people died where they fell, suffocated by the blanket of ash.

Italy

Pompeii

The sudden eruption of Vesuvius was disastrous. Within hours Pompeii was buried under five metres of ash and pumice.

Mount Vesuvius
Spewed out fire, smoke and ash

Fiery cloud
Ash drifted towards Pompeii

Fiorelli's plaster casts

When the people of Pompeii died, ash coated their bodies. Flesh and clothing decayed, leaving only the bones, but each body left a hollow **mould** in the ash. In 1860, Italian archaeologist Giuseppe Fiorelli pumped **plaster** into the spaces to make casts, and then dug out the casts. The plaster casts showed desperate people covering their eyes, children hiding in a cellar and even a dog trapped by its chain.

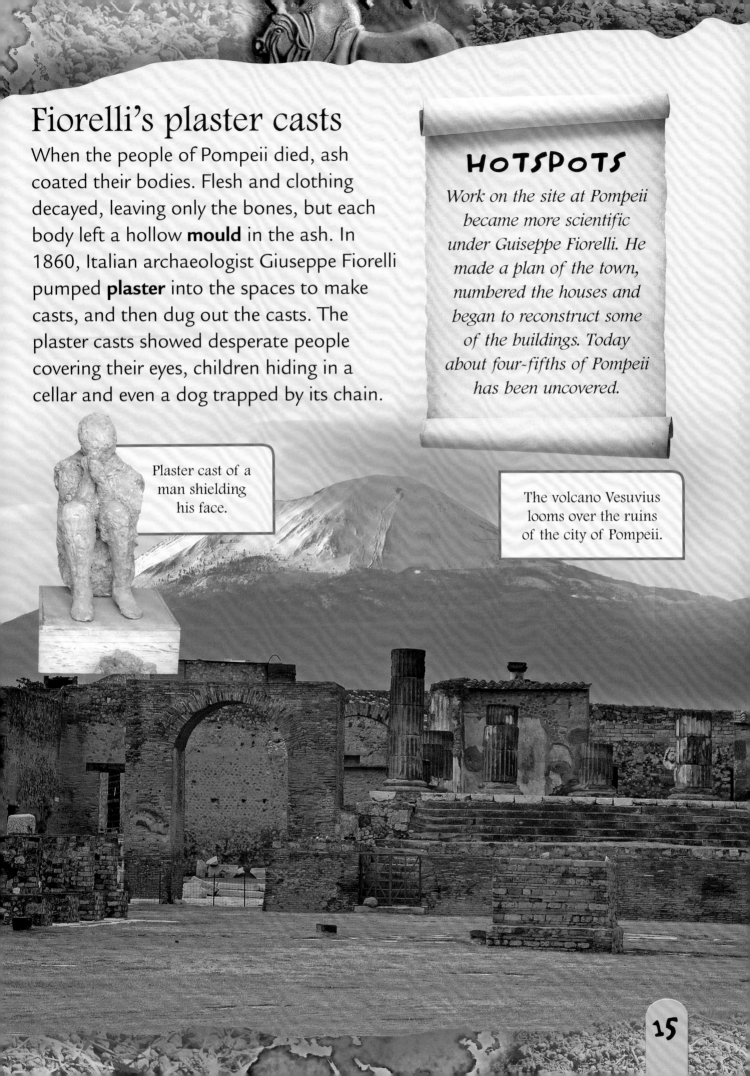

HOTSPOTS

Work on the site at Pompeii became more scientific under Guiseppe Fiorelli. He made a plan of the town, numbered the houses and began to reconstruct some of the buildings. Today about four-fifths of Pompeii has been uncovered.

Plaster cast of a man shielding his face.

The volcano Vesuvius looms over the ruins of the city of Pompeii.

Angkor

The ruined city of Angkor in Cambodia was the capital of the powerful Khmer empire between the 9th and the 14th centuries. By AD 1000 more than half a million people lived there.

Temple to Vishnu

In 1850, a French missionary hacked his way through dense jungle in Cambodia and stumbled across the ruins of a city with hundreds of temples and monuments. He had discovered the city of Angkor with its fascinating temple of Angkor Wat. The temple was built by King Suryavarman II for the Hindu god, Vishnu.

China

Cambodia
Angkor •

The temple of Angkor Wat seen from the moat. Two sets of walls and the moat cut the temple off from the city of Angkor. The five towers, shaped like lotus buds, rise to a height of 60 metres.

Angkor Wat

No one knows what happened to the people of Angkor or why the city was abandoned. Over many years the magnificent building of Angkor Wat was buried under the roots of huge trees growing in the jungle. When the temple was rediscovered, local people believed that it had been built by giants or gods. The five towers shaped like **lotus** buds stand for the five peaks at Mount Meru, a holy mountain from Hindu mythology which is at the centre of the universe and home of the Hindu gods.

HOTSPOTS

Some wall carvings show kings and soldiers going into battle on elephants. Their tusks had sharp metal points for inflicting extra damage. Other carvings show the massive heads of rulers or heavenly dancers.

The sculptures and decorative carvings of figures on the walls of Angkor Wat retell ancient myths.

Teotihuacan

The **Aztecs** discovered the ruins of one of the largest cities of ancient Mexico in the 14th century. They named it Teotihuacan, 'place of the gods'.

Street of the Dead

No one knows who lived in Teotihuacan or what happened to them. At its most powerful, around AD 600, more than 200,000 people may have lived there. This city of wide streets, pyramids, palaces, markets, workshops and houses was laid out in a grid pattern. At the centre of the city was a wide avenue which the Aztecs called the Street of the Dead. They wrongly thought that its buildings were the tombs of ancient gods.

NORTH AMERICA

Mexico

Teotihuacan

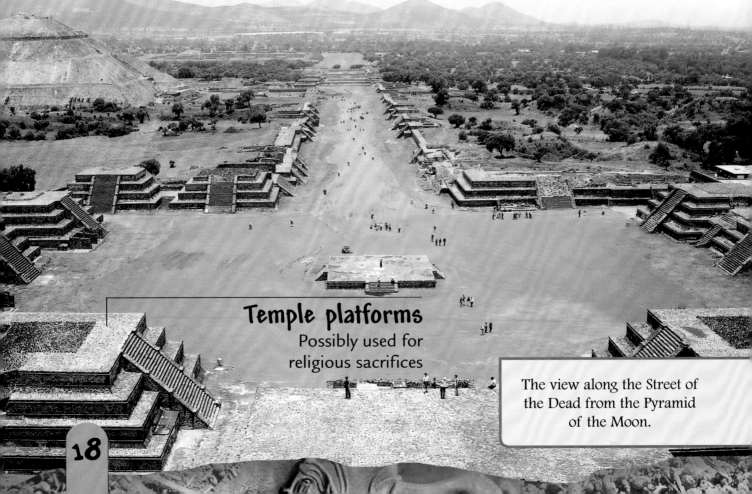

Temple platforms
Possibly used for religious sacrifices

The view along the Street of the Dead from the Pyramid of the Moon.

Sun, Moon and serpent

At the south end of the
Street of the Dead stands
the Pyramid of the Sun. It
was built on top of a large
cave where the Teotihuacanos
believed the world was formed.
On certain days of the year, the
Sun rises precisely to the east of
the pyramid, passes overhead, and
sets exactly to the west. There are
two other pyramids in the city,
the Pyramid of the Moon and the
Pyramid of the Feathered Serpent.

The Pyramid of the Sun is 65 metres high and
was built to honour the birth of the Sun god.

HOTSPOTS

*There is an Aztec myth that
tells how the Aztecs were
told by God to build a city
where they saw an eagle
sitting on a cactus eating
a snake. Today, a picture
of a snake and a cactus
are in the centre of
the Mexican flag.*

Great Zimbabwe

The remaining granite walls of Great Zimbabwe stand in the African country named after these ruins. Archaeologists believe that the site was the centre of a great African empire for hundreds of years.

Stone houses

Zimbabwe means 'stone houses'. The oldest ruins of Great Zimbabwe date from the 8th century, and the simple stone walls were probably put up 200 years later. Most of the buildings were built by the Shona people, who ruled the region between the late 13th and mid-15th centuries. Great Zimbabwe was a city of about 18,000 people, including miners, craftworkers and gold traders.

AFRICA

Zimbabwe

Great Zimbabwe •

A cone-shaped tower stands inside the walls of the Great Enclosure. No one knows what the tower was used for.

Stone blocks

Laid in straight rows to build up the tower

Part of the walls of the Great Enclosure. The ruins of more than 300 structures have so far been found inside.

The walls

Stone blocks laid in rows on top of each other without any **mortar**

Seven of these birds made of soapstone were found at the site.

The Great Enclosure

The main structure is a stone enclosure about 250 metres around. Its outer wall is ten metres high. Three narrow gaps lead to an interior, divided by further stone walls. Inside are the remains of many small mud buildings. Close to the wall stands a solid, ten-metre high cone-shaped tower without an entrance. We do not know what this was used for. It is shaped like a grain store so perhaps it was used in harvest ceremonies.

El Dorado

When Spanish explorers conquered Central and South America in the 16th century, they heard tales of a mysterious land of great wealth ruled by a golden king – and set off to find it.

The golden man

The Spaniards called the mysterious king El Dorado, 'the golden man'. They heard about a ceremony performed by the Chibcha people at a lake high in the Andes. It was said that every new Chibcha ruler was sprinkled with gold dust. Then he was rowed to the middle of a **sacred** lake on a raft loaded with gold and jewels. The king dived in, washing off the gold, while the treasures were thrown into the water for the Sun god.

Lake
• Guatavita

Colombia

SOUTH AMERICA

Attendants smeared the king's body with sticky earth and then blew gold dust over him.

Golden chiefs
Four local chiefs
accompanied
the king

Golden man
The king who was
rowed out on
to the lake

This gold model of the king's
reed raft was found in a cave
in Colombia in 1969. It is
19 centimetres long.

Treasure lake

The Spanish explorers set off in search
of gold. They found Lake Guatavita in
present-day Colombia. They drained the
lake and found emeralds and gold discs
in the mud. Hundreds of years later, in
1904, an English company recovered a
golden helmet, and in the 1960s another
team arrived with suction pumps to search
for more treasure. But the Colombian
government of the time put an end to the
treasure hunt and placed the lake under
national protection. Many people believe
that gold still lies beneath its waters.

HOTSPOTS

*In 1595, Walter Raleigh set
off from England in search of
El Dorado. He sailed up the
Orinoco in South America
and made friends with
a Native American chief.
Raleigh hoped the chief
would lead him up the
golden path, but he
was disappointed.*

Tikal

The jungles of Guatemala hide the ruins of a network of ancient Maya cities. In 1848 explorers found the Maya capital of Tikal. The king and his nobles lived here in stone palaces in the heart of the capital.

High-rise temples

When Tikal was at its most powerful, around AD 700, it had palaces, temples and tall pyramids all painted in bright colours. Priests performed ceremonies in the temple and deer, dogs and turkeys were sacrificed to the gods. At royal funerals humans were also sacrificed.

A wide stone stairway leads to the temple platform at the top of the pyramid.

NORTH
AMERICA

Guatemala •Tikal

SOUTH
AMERICA

Fun and games

Each city had a ball court. Two teams of players tried to hit a large ball through a stone ring mounted high on the wall. They hit the ball, which was not allowed to touch the floor, with their forearms, shoulders, elbows and hips, but not with their hands. For the Maya the game was a sacred ritual. The losers were sometimes killed by priests, and their blood sacrificed to the gods.

Stone hoop

The ball had to pass through a hoop which was about six metres off the ground

This stone slab, called a stela, recorded important dates in the life of a Mayan ruler.

The ball court was shaped like a capital I. Women are also thought to have played the game. They wore extra padding on their stomach and legs.

Machu Picchu

In 1911 the American archaeologist Hiram Bingham (1875–1956) discovered the haunting ruins of an **Inca** citadel. This was Machu Picchu, perched high on a mountain ridge in the Peruvian Andes.

Away from it all

Machu Picchu was probably built as a royal **retreat** for the Inca ruler and his family. The palaces, ceremonial buildings, baths and temples were built higher up the mountain. Stone houses for farmers, weavers and servants were built on the lower terraces.

Peru • **Machu Picchu**

SOUTH
AMERICA

Machu Picchu lies at a height of 2,350 metres. It was so well hidden that the Spanish invaders failed to find it.

Sun worshippers

The Intihuatana ('hitching post of the sun') was a sacred column of stone dedicated to the Inca sun god, Inti. Here animals and children were sacrificed to the god, to make sure he never disappeared. The Inca priests also used the stone column as a sundial. In front of it lay the Temple of Three Windows, which might have been an astronomical observatory.

The Intihuatana Stone at Machu Picchu. This important religious site was where the Incas held many ceremonies.

Stone pillar
At midday on 21 March and 21 September, the Sun is directly above the pillar

Finding lost cities

Are there more lost cities still to be found? No one knows for sure, but many experts believe that there may be more to be discovered.

The mystery of Atlantis

In about 360 BC, the ancient Greek philosopher Plato wrote about a legendary island **civilization** called Atlantis. Legend said that the island had exploded and sunk beneath the waves. People have searched for Atlantis ever since, but without success. Some believe it was really the Mediterranean island of Thira (also called Santorini), where there was an enormous volcanic **eruption** in about 1470 BC.

Greece

•Thira

The crescent-shaped caldera at Thira. This is where the volcano collapsed into the sea after it erupted.

A new beginning?

If we discover more lost cities in future, we might find even older civilizations than those we know about today. Some historians believe there could have been a 'mother culture' that came before the earliest cities of Mesopotamia. Their people might have taught the Egyptians and Maya how to build pyramids. Who knows? Perhaps future finds will tell us.

This statue was found underwater near one of the possible Atlantis sites.

HOTSPOTS

Modern archaeologists use space age technology in their search for lost cities. They look at satellite images of deserts and rainforests to see if they can spot any odd or unusual features on the ground that might point to a hidden city.

Underwater archaeology – divers search the sea bed for evidence of more lost cities.

Glossary

archaeologist A person who studies the ancient past by digging up and looking at remains.

Aztecs The Native American people who dominated Mexico before the Spanish arrived in the 16th century.

besiege To surround (a city) to force its people to surrender.

bitumen A sticky mixture, like tar.

caldera A large crater (bowl-shaped hollow) in a volcano.

citadel A fortress that protects a city.

civilization A large group of people who live and work together, to build a society in which science, the arts and a form of government are produced.

decipher To work out what words or symbols mean.

eruption The violent explosion when a volcano throws out ash, red-hot rock, smoke and other material.

excavate To dig to find ancient remains.

grid A network or criss-cross system.

gut Thin cord made from animal parts.

Incas The Native American people of the Andes Mountains of South America.

Indus gods The gods worshipped by people living in the Indus Valley in Pakistan. The gods were linked to agriculture and to the earth as the giver of life.

labyrinth A maze, or series of paths, that it is difficult to find a way through.

lotus A beautiful water lily.

Maya The Native American people of Central America.

Minoans People of the ancient civilization of Crete (named after their king, Minos).

Minotaur A mythical creature with the body of a man and the head of a bull.

mortar A cement-like mixture used to hold stones or bricks together.

mould The shape or form of something.

mural A picture painted on a wall (or pyramid).

plaster A liquid paste that is hard and smooth when it dries.

pumice A very light, porous rock.

retreat A place where people go for peace and quiet.

ritual To do with ceremonial or religious practices.

sacred Dedicated to a god or serving a religious purpose.

seal A closure for a package of goods or a letter.

settlement A small community of people.

soapstone A soft kind of stone that is easy to carve.

stela (plural stelae) An upright stone slab that was engraved with words and pictures.

tablet A small slab of stone or clay.

ziggurat A pyramid-shaped, stepped tower.

Index

Webfinder

www.culture.gr – Presenting Knossos and other Greek sites.

www.harcourtschool.com/activity/pompeii – Learn much more about Pompeii.

www.smm.org/sln/ma/index.html – A Maya Adventure, including information about Tikal.

www.unmuseum.org/lostcity.htm – Facts on Machu Picchu and other lost cities.

news.bbc.co.uk/1/hi/england/1923794.stm – Story of a recently discovered lost city.

news.bbc.co.uk/1/hi/sci/tech/3766863.stm – Could this be Atlantis?